D0896117

cooking with
Essential Oils

CHEF JOHN O'NEIL

Copyright © 2019. Chef John Media, LLC.

All rights reserved. No part of this work may be reproduced or copied in any form or by any means – graphic, electronic, or mechanical, including photocopying, recording, taping, or information and retrieval systems – without written permission of the publisher.

ISBN: 978-1-7342508-6-2

Printed in the United States of America

For additional information, contact:

Chef John O'Neil
john@chefjohnoneil.com
Chef John Media, LLC
5323 Spring Valley Road Suite 150 Dallas, Texas 75254
Tel: (972) 852-8000
Fax: (214) 306-7830
www.chefjohnoneil.com

CONTENTS

INTRODUCTION

First, I'll tell you a little bit about how I came to use essential oils for cooking. We discovered essential oils for aromatherapy many years ago. We were accustomed to using lavender aromatically or eucalyptus topically. I never considered how essential oils could both enhance wellness and improve food flavors by using them in cooking. But when I discovered them... WOW! A whole new world opened up for me! I've been a chef for over 20 years, classically trained and educated. I use fresh and dried herbs and other spices in cooking. The first time I put a couple of drops of lemon essential oil in a vinaigrette dressing, I was a solid believer. I just didn't know what I didn't know, and now my eyes have been opened to a new realm of flavors.

I continue to be amazed at how these concentrated little drops can POP the flavor to bring life to old recipes. At first, I only used the oils in cold preparations to maintain the integrity of the wellness properties of the oils. Then, I experimented with them in warm foods and baking. While the heat cooks out many of the health-enhancing properties, the flavor explosion remains.

The first time I made peppermint brownies using the oils, I could not believe what my mouth was telling me! I could never get peppermint brownies to have a strong enough mint flavor. It just wasn't worth the effort when using fresh or dried mint. Even mint extract or liquor paled. A couple of drops of peppermint essential oil made the difference!

I set out trying other favorite dishes that I've made for years and gave them new life using oils. Individual flavors can either be subdued or brought to the front based on what you want to achieve. Building layers of flavors using the oils in combination with fresh and dried herbs and spices, tried-and-true family recipes were reincarnated with depth and dimension. Then, try reversing the oil-to-herb emphasis the next time you make that dish to reverse the flavor profile for a completely different experience.

When using essential oils for cooking, I insist that you use only the most natural and purest essential oils. While the Food and Drug Administration has a list of essential oils that are "generally recognized as safe," very few brands of oils out there are as "pure" as the labeling leads you to believe. If the labeling on the oil bottle cautions against internal use, do not use it for cooking. Due to the laxity of U.S. regulations for labeling essential oils, you cannot be sure what is really in the bottle.

ABOUT THE CHEF

For internal use in cooking, do your own research. Choose a brand from a company with integrity and transparency in their production that assures you that there really is only essential oil, and nothing else, in the bottle. I have chosen to use Young Living's Vitality line of essential oils in my kitchen and in this book. They are the only company that I know of that has a separate line of oils with labeling indicating the FDA's approval to use that oil for internal consumption and in cooking. I trust their process and believe in the quality of their essential oils.

Two final tips before we dive into the recipes. First, the essential oils are very potent. It is easy to use too much and overpower your dish. If you are experimenting with oils in one of your own recipes, start using the toothpick method of adding the oils to control the amount. The toothpick method means you dip the toothpick into the essential oil and swirl the toothpick residue into your dish. You can always add more, but if you use too much, it will be impossible to go back from that. On the other hand, don't be afraid to experiment with the oils in your dishes. Believe me, I had many dishes that were inedible during the creation of this book because I got "drop-happy" and used too much. But, some of the dishes surprised me when I experimented, so I would never have learned otherwise.

I hope you enjoy this book as much as I have enjoyed creating it. The process of making this book meant creating new recipes and refining old ones, having many dinner parties to test the oil-infused dishes on friends and family, and spending many hours at local coffee houses writing the how-to for you to be able to recreate them at home. It has been some of the most pleasurable times of my professional chef career!

Chef John

ABOUT ESSENTIAL OILS

What are essential oils?
When you smell the unique scent of a rose or smell the scent of cedar in the Central Texas countryside, you are smelling the powerful effect of essential oils. Essential oils are much more than just pleasant scents. They are powerful plant extracts that promote greater wellness.

Essential oils come from steam distillation or the cold pressing of plant material, separating the essential oils from the water and plant materials. Essential oils can be used in the home as a non-toxic alternative to chemical cleaning products. They can also be used promote the body's natural health and wellness in several different ways—physical health, beauty regimen, and emotional support.

How do you use essential oils?
There are three ways to use essential oils—aromatically, topically, and internally. When essential oils are used aromatically, this involves either direct inhalation by, for example, putting an oil on your hands and smelling it, or by using a diffuser to cold steam the oils into the air. The study of using essential oils aromatically is called aromatherapy and is the most common method of using essential oils. During inhalation, essential oils absorb into the body through the respiratory system.

Essential oils can also be used topically by rubbing the oil, usually diluted in a carrier oil, on the skin. This way, the oil is absorbed into the skin which transfers the oil into the bloodstream. When oils are used topically on the bottoms of the feet, the feet's large pores allow for rapid absorption into the body.

Internal consumption of essential oils is less common, at least as far as most people know. Many processed foods use essential oils in their flavorings—think chewing gum, chocolates, candies, and many more. The Federal Drug Administration has approved many essential oils for internal consumption, giving these oils the status of "generally regarded as safe."

Are there differences in the quality of oils?
There are many differences in the quality of essential oils available on the market. Essential oils are expensive to produce because of the amount of plant material that is required to get a small quantity of pure oil. To make the end product cheaper, some companies dilute the pure and natural essential oil with lab-created synthetics or alcohol-type adulterants. For this reason, it is important to research the company from which you buy oils.

Based on our research, we chose Young Living, the oldest essential oil company in America, as the company we trust to provide pure, unadulterated essential oils. Young Living's founder Gary D. Young started the essential oil movement in America. The company guarantees the purity and quality of their oils both through in-house and third-party testing.

What are the basics of cooking with essential oils?
Essential oils can be up to 70% stronger than their fresh and dried herb counterparts since fresh and dried herbs only retain about 5-10% of the essential oils from the original plant. Essential oils are superior in flavor and potency over dried herbs and have a longer shelf life. Never fear, fresh and dried herbs still have a place in cooking because of the nutrients they offer and the differences in taste and texture from essential oils.
Essential oils are a very concentrated portion of the original plant material, so they should be used in smaller quantities than the whole plant substance.

It is also a good idea to dilute the essential oils into a carrier oil (like olive oil) or a syrup before adding it to a recipe. This ensures that the essential oil gets mixed into the whole dish.

Lastly, essential oils are "volatile," which means that they are fragile and dissipate in high heat. In order to maintain the maximum healthful properties of the essential oils, use them in cold-applications. When using essential oils in hot preparations, add them at the end of the preparation, if possible. Otherwise, you can expect to lose a bit of the properties in the cooking process. Even so, the essential oils will still provide enhanced flavors in the cooking and maintain some of the healthful properties.

What's the difference between essential oils and vegetable oils?
Vegetable oils are fats, pressed from seeds and nuts or the bran of grains. They contain glycerol, which is the greasy residue and slippery surface characteristic of such fatty oils. Essential oils contain no fat and are mostly steam distilled from plant material.

What's the difference between essential oils and extracts?
To make an extract, plant material is soaked in a liquid (such as alcohol) in order to isolate or extract a certain amount of flavor from the plant. Liquid extracts are used as flavoring in cooking, as perfumes, or in medicines. Examples include vanilla extract, where vanilla beans are soaked in alcohol, which is used in baking.

The process of obtaining essential oils is much more complex, through steam distillation. The liquid that is distilled off is called a plant essence and the very small amount of volatile liquid left behind is the essential oil. It requires a large amount of plant material to obtain a small amount of essential oil, but the essential oil is much more potent than a liquid extract.

What is the ratio for substituting essential oils for fresh or dried herbs?
While there is no bright line rule for substituting essential oils for fresh or dried herbs, a good rule of thumb is one drop of essential oil is approximately one teaspoon of fresh or dried herbs.

What essential oils are approved for internal consumption by the FDA?
The Federal Drug Administration approves of certain essential oils as generally recognized as safe for internal consumption. The Code of Federal Regulations provides the list of food substances generally recognized as safe for human consumption. [Citation: 21 CFR 182.20.] Young Living has worked with the FDA to develop and package certain essential oils for internal consumption – called their Vitality Line.

These include: Basil Vitality, Lemongrass Vitality, Oregano Vitality, Rosemary Vitality, Thyme Vitality, Lavender Vitality, Peppermint Vitality, Spearmint Vitality, Laurus Nobilis Vitality, Mountain Savory Vitality, Marjoram Vitality, Sage Vitality, German Chamomile Vitality, Tarragon Vitality, Black Pepper Vitality, Cinnamon Bark Vitality, Clove Vitality, Ginger Vitality, Carrot Seed Vitality, Celery Seed Vitality, Dill Vitality, Cardamom Vitality, Coriander Vitality, Nutmeg Vitality, Fennel Vitality, Bergamot Vitality, Grapefruit Vitality, Jade Lemon Vitality, Lemon Vitality, Lime Vitality, Orange Vitality, and Tangerine Vitality.

Recipes

Black Bean Avocado Salad

I originally got this recipe from my sister Corey when she made it for a baby shower. I immediately fell in in love with the simplicity of it. Then, I added essential oils and it went to another level!

– Chef John

INGREDIENTS

1 CAN BLACK BEANS, DRAINED AND RINSED

1 1/4 CUP FROZEN CORN

1 CUP RED PEPPER, DICED

3/4 CUP RED ONION, DICED

1 ROMA TOMATO, DICED

1/4 CUP COTIJA CHEESE, CRUMBLED

1 MEDIUM AVOCADO, DICED

3 TABLESPOONS RED WINE VINEGAR

3 TABLESPOONS OLIVE OIL

5 DROPS BLACK PEPPER ESSENTIAL OIL

3 DROPS LIME ESSENTIAL OIL

1 TEASPOON GROUND BLACK PEPPER

1 TEASPOON SALT

OPTIONAL: 1 SERRANO PEPPER, FINELY CHOPPED

DIRECTIONS

Add all ingredients to a medium mixing bowl and mix to incorporate. Adjust seasoning with salt and pepper to your taste. Depending on the size of the avocado used, you may want to add another teaspoon or two of red wine vinegar.

Blueberry Lemony Coffee Cake

My mother was born in Maine, where they grow blueberries wild. The blueberries in Maine are small and super sweet. One year my wife and I went to Maine on vacation and to visit family. We found a co-op packer that had frozen blueberries for sale. I want you to know that my wife and I went to a store and found a 50-quart cooler, filled it with frozen blueberries, duct taped it shut, and check it like luggage. I put a note on top inside the cooler that asked TSA to please reseal the cooler when they opened it. And, they did! They were still frozen when we got them to Texas. We had blueberries in the freezer for years!

This recipe comes from my grandmother, Jeanne Corson. The area of Maine they came from is called "down east" Maine. So, the original recipe is called Down-East Blueberry Cake. Lemon and blueberry are flavors that go well together, so I adapted this recipe to add lemon essential oil. You will be amazed at how the flavor just jumps out at you!

– Chef John

INGREDIENTS

1 CUP PLUS 1/4 CUP SUGAR, DIVIDED

1/2 TSP SALT

2 DROPS CINNAMON BARK ESSENTIAL OIL

1/2 CUP BUTTER, SOFTENED (1 STICK)

2 EGGS (WHOLE)

1/4 TEASPOON GROUND NUTMEG

1/4 TEASPOON GROUND CINNAMON

1 TEASPOON VANILLA

2 CUPS PLUS 2 TABLESPOONS ALL-PURPOSE FLOUR

2 TEASPOONS BAKING POWDER

1/2 CUP CANNED EVAPORATED MILK

1 1/4 CUPS FRESH OR FROZEN WILD MAINE BLUEBERRIES

4 DROPS OF LEMON ESSENTIAL OIL

NOTE ABOUT BLUEBERRIES

Tossing the blueberries in flour helps with two things: first, the blueberries won't all fall to the bottom of the pan; second, it helps to not turn the entire cake a purplish-gray color. Wild Maine blueberries and most Canadian blueberries are very small and very sweet. Because of this, they run very fast. It is important that you not mix the flour with them until right before you need to add them to the recipe. If you do this too soon, they will get very runny.

DIRECTIONS

Preheat oven to 350 degrees. Mix the 2 cups of flour and baking powder and salt together and set aside. Cream together 1 cup of the sugar, butter, eggs, and cinnamon bark essential oil for about 2 minutes on medium speed. Add milk and vanilla and mix for another minute, scraping the sides of the bowl. Add flour and baking powder and mix until all of the ingredients are incorporated.

In a medium-sized mixing bowl, add lemon essential oil by dropping it around the sides of the bowl about 2 inches from the bottom. Add the blueberries to the bowl and toss for about 30 seconds to mix the essential oil into the blueberries. Next, add the 2 tablespoons of flour and lightly toss to coat blueberries. With a wooden or nonstick spoon, fold in blueberries into batter, just enough to incorporate. Pour into a well-greased 9x13 pan. Combine the 1/4 cup sugar, nutmeg, and cinnamon and sprinkle over the top of the batter.

Bake about 40 minutes until done.

Chai Latte Mixer

I fell in love with chai when I worked in Boulder, Colorado. In the cold weather, a warm chai makes you feel good on the inside. Essential oils pair well to make a chai mixer. I like to use non-dairy milk substitute (like pea protein milk) for this recipe because it will stay fresher and last longer in the refrigerator than using regular milk. By not using dairy in this recipe, the Mixer freezes very well for up to a month or so. Just put some in a small Mason jar for the refrigerator and put the rest in small Mason jars to freeze and use next week and the next.

— Chef John

INGREDIENTS

2 CUPS HONEY

1/4 CUP MOLASSES

1 1/2 QUARTS MILK OR MILK SUBSTITUTE

2 OUNCES FRESH GRATED GINGER

2 TABLESPOONS GROUND CINNAMON

1 TABLESPOON GROUND NUTMEG

1 TEASPOON GROUND GINGER

1 TEASPOON GROUND ALLSPICE

1/2 TEASPOON GROUND CLOVE

2 DROPS CINNAMON BARK ESSENTIAL OIL

2 DROPS NUTMEG ESSENTIAL OIL

1 DROP CLOVE ESSENTIAL OIL

4 DROPS CARDAMOM ESSENTIAL OIL

DIRECTIONS

In blender, place grated ginger with 1/2 of the milk and puree in order to eliminate the ginger chunks. Pour ginger mix into stock pot, add remaining milk and remaining ground spices. Bring to simmer but DO NOT BOIL! Turn off heat and let cool to room temperature in pot for about an hour. Add essential oils after it has cooled. Pour all liquid in a pitcher or in sealed mason jars and place in fridge. Will keep for about 2 weeks.

NOTE GROUND SPICES

Ground spices sitting in little containers in your pantry should be replaced every 6 months or so. They lose their potency and flavor after a short while. A whole spice, like cinnamon bark or black peppercorns will last about a year in their whole form. While using spices beyond this period will not likely hurt you, it will not provide the flavor that you seek in your dish. It is best to get small amounts of spices and use them when you buy them instead of buying in bulk and keeping the spices for a long time. I like to buy small amounts of ground spices in the bulk section of the grocery store to use immediately in whatever I'm cooking at that time.

Hot Chai Tea Latte

DIRECTIONS

Heat one cup of Chai Latte Mixer to warm (not boiling). Add one cup of hot black tea and mix.

Iced Chai Tea Latte

DIRECTIONS

Mix equal parts cold black tea and Chai Latte Mixer and serve over ice.

Coffee Chai Latte

DIRECTIONS

Heat 1 1/2 cups Chai Latte Mixer to warm (not boiling). Add 1/2 cup of super strong black coffee and mix. (I like to use undiluted coffee toddy coffee for this!)

Dirty Chai Latte

DIRECTIONS

Heat 1 cup Chai Latte Mixer to warm (not boiling). Add a double shot of espresso.

Chimichurri Steak Salad

Chimichurri is a light, oil-based condiment with origins in Argentina. The name comes from a Spanish Basque word that means "a mixture of several things in no particular order." In South America, each family has their own version of a chimichurri recipe handed down over centuries. I like it because it is bright and fresh with a ridiculous amount of flavor. Plus, it is great to use throughout all of the dishes for an entire meal. One tip, though—rough chop the parsley and cilantro by hand. If you use a food processor the herbs will turn to puree and you will end up with baby food instead of a condiment or sauce.

— Chef John

CHIMICHURRI SAUCE

6 CLOVES GARLIC, PEELED AND CHOPPED

2 TEASPOONS RED CHILI FLAKES (CRUSHED RED PEPPER)

1 CUP PLUS 6 TABLESPOONS EXTRA VIRGIN OLIVE OIL OR ANY LIGHT, NEUTRAL OIL

1 CUP PACKED CILANTRO LEAVES (ABOUT 2 BUNCHES), ROUGH CHOPPED BY HAND

2 CUPS PACKED FLAT LEAF PARSLEY (ABOUT 4 BUNCHES), ROUGH CHOPPED BY HAND

1 TABLESPOON FRESH LEMON VERBENA HERB, ROUGH CHOPPED BY HAND

1 TABLESPOON FRESH OREGANO, ROUGH CHOPPED BY HAND

1 TABLESPOON FRESH THYME, ROUGH CHOPPED BY HAND

1 SERRANO CHILE, CHOPPED

1/2 CUP RED WINE VINEGAR

1 LEMON, ZESTED THEN JUICED

3 DROPS LEMON ESSENTIAL OIL

5 DROPS PARSLEY ESSENTIAL OIL

2 DROPS CILANTRO ESSENTIAL OIL

SALT AND PEPPER TO TASTE

DIRECTIONS

Heat 6 tablespoons of the oil until just warm to touch, maybe about 100-110 degrees. Add chili flakes and garlic. Remove from heat and let it sit for one minute. Add rest of the oil and set aside.

Wash and dry fresh herbs. Rough chop with a sharp, large knife by hand. (I do not recommend using a food processor because the result will be a puree.)

Add all remaining ingredients to a large Mason jar with a tight lid. Shake well and refrigerate for an hour.

Chimichurri Marinated Flatiron Steak

INGREDIENTS

1 1/3 POUNDS FLATIRON STEAK
6 SHALLOTS CUT IN HALF
1 CUP CHIMICHURRI SAUCE (PREVIOUS PAGE)

DIRECTIONS

Pour chimichurri sauce on steak in pan and lay shallots on top. Let sit for at least 3 hours up to 5 hours. Remove steak from marinade and grill for 3-4 minutes. Then, put steak back in pan and finish in 350 degree oven for 10-12 minutes.

Chimichurri Marinated Zucchini

INGREDIENTS

1 YELLOW SQUASH, SLICED LENGTHWISE
1 ZUCCHINI, SLICED LENGTHWISE
1/4 CUP CHIMICHURRI SAUCE (PREVIOUS PAGE)
2 DROPS BLACK PEPPER ESSENTIAL OIL

DIRECTIONS

Put squash, sauce, and essential oil in zip-top bag and marinate for an hour. Grill for 2 minutes per side. Brush with remaining sauce.

Chimichurri Marinated Tomatoes

INGREDIENTS

1/4 CUP CHIMICHURRI SAUCE (PREVIOUS PAGE)

2 TABLESPOONS OREGANO ESSENTIAL OIL

3 DROPS BLACK PEPPER ESSENTIAL OIL

1 DROP LEMON ESSENTIAL OIL

2 LARGE HEIRLOOM TOMATOES, CHOPPED (OR 4 CUPS CHOPPED). (I LIKE CHEROKEE PURPLE HEIRLOOM TOMATOES WHEN IN SEASON.)

2 OUNCES SHAVED MANCHEGO CHEESE (I PREFER A HARDER, AGED MANCHEGO.)

DIRECTIONS

Place 1/4 cup chimichurri sauce, essential oils, and tomatoes in a bowl and marinate a couple of hours. Place on a plate for serving. Drizzle with remaining sauce and cheese.

Chimichurri Vinaigrette

INGREDIENTS

1/2 CUP CHIMICHURRI SAUCE (PREVIOUS PAGE)
1 TEASPOON MUSTARD
1 TABLESPOON HONEY
1 MEDIUM SHALLOT, SLICED
1/4 CUP OLIVE OIL

2 TABLESPOONS RED WINE VINEGAR
2 DROPS OREGANO ESSENTIAL OIL
2 DROPS LEMON ESSENTIAL OIL
2 DROPS THYME ESSENTIAL OIL

DIRECTIONS

Place all ingredients in a shaker cup and shake well to combine. Refrigerate.

Chimichurri Meat Drizzle

INGREDIENTS

1/4 CUP CHIMICHURRI SAUCE (PREVIOUS PAGE)

2 DROPS OREGANO ESSENTIAL OIL

2 DROPS BLACK PEPPER ESSENTIAL OIL

1 DROP LEMON ESSENTIAL OIL

2 DROPS ROSEMARY ESSENTIAL OIL

DIRECTIONS

Combine all ingredients in shaker cup and shake well to combine. Spoon over grilled flatiron steak when served.

Chimichurri Grilled Salad

INGREDIENTS

2 CUPS BABY ARUGULA
2 HEADS ROMAINE LETTUCE, CUT IN HALF
2 OUNCES SHAVED MANCHEGO CHEESE

CHIMICHURRI VINAIGRETTE (ABOVE)
4 SLICES ITALIAN RUSTIC BREAD

DIRECTIONS

Brush cut-side of Romaine lettuce with Chimichurri Vinaigrette. Place cut side down on oven burner or grill for a count of 10. (This goes by very quickly. You just want the char for flavor.) Chop grilled lettuce and arugula together. Mix half of cheese into chopped salad mix. Toss with Chimichurri Vinaigrette.

Grill bread on oven burner then put in oven to finish for 5 minutes to make crisp like a crouton.

To serve, lay grilled bread down on plate, top with salad, sprinkle with remaining cheese.

Chimichurri Flatiron Steak Salad

DIRECTIONS

Putting the whole meal together, lay grilled bread on plate. Top with grilled salad mix. Lay sliced zucchini on top of grilled salad mix. Spoon marinated tomatoes and cheese over salad mix. Slice flatiron steak and lay on top of tomatoes. Lastly, drizzle with Chimichurri Meat Drizzle and salt and pepper to taste.

NOTE ABOUT VINAIGRETTES

A basic vinaigrette is just a 3:1 ratio of 3 parts oil to 1 part vinegar. I love to use olive oil. For the vinegar, don't use white vinegar. Some vinegars I love to have on hand are red or white wine, apple cider, rice wine, fruit vinegars of any kind, lemon or any citrus juice or balsamic. Your ratio will vary slightly based on the acidity. For example, rice wine vinegar, balsamic vinegar, and lime juice are moderately low in acidity and higher in sugar so you might have to add a little more to balance the flavors.

Chocolate Orange Truffles

This is my wife's favorite thing for Valentine's Day. I only make these for special occasions because they are so decadent. I recommend buying the highest quality chocolate you can find. It may take a trip to a specialty store. The better the chocolate, the better these are. The orange flavor is so unexpected with the chocolate. You can substitute peppermint essential oil for the orange essential oil, if you prefer. The second coating of chocolate is meant to give the outer hard shell that pops when you bite into it with the soft center. Don't overheat the chocolate in this step.

– Chef John

INGREDIENTS

5 OUNCES SEMI-SWEET CHOCOLATE CHIPS

5 OUNCES MILK CHOCOLATE CHIPS

3 TABLESPOONS UNSALTED BUTTER

1/4 CUP HEAVY CREAM

3 TABLESPOONS CREAM CHEESE

1 TABLESPOON LIGHT CORN SYRUP

1/4 CUP ORANGE LIQUEUR

10 DROPS ORANGE ESSENTIAL OIL

1/2 CUP DUTCH PROCESS COCOA POWDER

FINELY CHOPPED NUTS (I LIKE PISTACHIOS)

TOASTED FLAKED COCONUT

8 OUNCES SEMI-SWEET OR BITTERSWEET CHOCOLATE, CHOPPED FINE

DIRECTIONS

Place the 10 ounces of chocolate chips, butter and cream cheese in a medium sized glass mixing bowl. Microwave on 50% power for 30 seconds. (Do not use high power.) Remove and stir. Repeat this process 1 more time. Set aside.

Heat the heavy cream and corn syrup in a small saucepan over medium heat until it just starts to simmer. Remove from the heat and pour the cream mixture over the melted chocolate mixture. DO NOT STIR—let it stand for at least a minute, but no longer than 2 minutes. Using a flexible spatula, gently stir starting in the middle of bowl and working in concentric circles until all chocolate is melted and mixture is smooth and creamy. Gently stir in the liqueur and the orange essential oil. Pour the mixture into an 8 by 8-inch glass baking dish and place in the refrigerator for 30 minutes.

Using a melon baller, scoop chocolate balls onto a sheet pan lined with parchment paper and return to the refrigerator for 30 minutes.

In the meantime, place the remaining 8 ounces of chocolate into a small crockpot type vessel set to medium heat. Stir the chocolate occasionally and test the temperature of the chocolate. Continue heating until it reaches just warm—90 - 92 degrees F; do not allow the chocolate to go above 94 degrees F. If you do, the outer chocolate shell will not have the right "pop" to it when you bite into the chocolate. Once you have reached the optimal temperature, adjust the heat to maintain it.

Place the cocoa powder, chopped nuts, and flaked coconut in separate bowls.

Remove the truffle from the refrigerator and shape into balls by rolling between the palms of your hands. Use powder-free vinyl or latex gloves, if desired.

Dip a large ladle into the chocolate and turn upside down to remove excess chocolate. Place truffles 1 at time into the scoop and using a fork roll around until coated. Place the coated truffle ball into the dish with either the cocoa powder, nuts, or coconut. Move the truffle around to coat; leave truffle in the coating for 10 to 15 seconds before removing. After 10 to 15 seconds, remove the truffle to a parchment lined sheet pan. Repeat until all truffles are coated. Allow to set in a cool dry place for at least 1 hour; or store in an airtight container in the refrigerator. These truffles are best when served at room temperature.

Cilantro Lime Flank Steak Tacos

These are a fun and easy party food. Flank steak is flavorful and tender. Serving the tacos in butter leaf lettuce makes the dish colorful and healthy. We first made these for a brunch oil party we had at the house. They were such a hit, everyone wanted the recipe. Well, folks, here it is!

— *Chef John*

LIME HONEY MARINADE

1/2 CUP SOY SAUCE
1/2 CUP HONEY
1/2 CUP VEGETABLE OIL
1/2 CUP THINLY SLICED GREEN ONIONS (GREEN PART ONLY—NO WHITE)

2 FLANK STEAKS WHOLE AND TRIMMED (CONNECTIVE TISSUE REMOVED)
2 DROPS LIME ESSENTIAL OIL

DIRECTIONS

To make marinade, in 2-quart sauce pot, bring soy sauce just to a boil and turn off heat. Add rest of the ingredients except the essential oil and stir until honey is melted. Set aside and cool to room temperature. Add the essential oil when cooled. You can put this in a Mason Jar and refrigerate to use later. Shake very well before using. Follow the ratios to increase the amount of this recipe. It freezes well and keeps for up to 4 months.

In a gallon size ziptop bag or larger (or large container with a sealable, leakproof lid) marinate flank steak with marinade (above) 8-10 hours or overnight. Preheat oven to 350 degrees. Line a baking sheet with aluminum foil. Remove steak from marinade and discard excess. Grill flank steak for 5 minutes per side, turning every 30 seconds or so. Place on aluminum foil lined pan and place in oven for 15 minutes. Remove and let rest for 20 minutes, then place in refrigerator for at least an hour before slicing. Slice very thin against the grain then turn meat 90 degrees and slice in the other direction making very small pieces.

CILANTRO LIME DRESSING

1/2 CUP CILANTRO, CHOPPED

ZEST AND JUICE OF ONE LIME

1 CLOVE GARLIC, SLICED

1 TABLESPOON HONEY

1/2 CUP OIL

5 DROPS CILANTRO ESSENTIAL OIL

1/2 TEASPOON SALT

1 TEASPOON BLACK PEPPER

3 TABLESPOONS MAYONNAISE

DIRECTIONS

Put all ingredients except mayonnaise in blender. Blend on high 10-15 seconds until smooth and creamy. Pour in medium size mixing bowl and whisk in mayonnaise. Add more salt and pepper to taste. Store in Mason jar in refrigerator.

NOTE "MASON" JARS

I love to use canning jars, plain and simple! Unless the jar breaks or chips, it will last forever. I use wide mouth and small mouth. I also use them for everyday drinking glasses.

A chef long ago taught me that a clean mason jar has a clean taste. He advised, plastic "breathes," meaning that plastic, polycarbonate containers, or baggies will absorb the volatile oils of your spices or the flavors of your vinegars. This is especially important for spices like clove, cumin, or ground chiles.

The average home cook might not use the spices for a few months, where a restaurant goes through a large quantity of spices. A home cook's spices have a high probability of going stale. Glass jars with metal lids, or containers that have locking lids with rubber rings that are in good condition will keep your spices, flours, sugars, vinaigrettes and such fresh for much longer. My rule is to use clean rings and lids for any food containing sugar or honey. Replacing rings and lids costs less than replacing plastic containers. I assure you, making a chocolate protein shake in a plastic shaker cup that had a red wine vinaigrette left in it for a few days will simply not taste the same.

Flank Steak Tacos

GARNISH DRIZZLE

1 1/4 CUP CILANTRO LIME DRESSING (PREVIOUS PAGE)
1 CUP FINELY CHOPPED RED BELL PEPPER
ZEST AND JUICE OF HALF A LIME
5 DROPS BLACK PEPPER ESSENTIAL OIL

2 DROPS LIME ESSENTIAL OIL
SALT AND PEPPER TO TASTE
COTIJA CHEESE

DIRECTIONS

To make tacos, place chopped flank steak in bowl and add just enough cilantro lime dressing to barely coat the meat. You can always add more but it is impossible to take away if you add too much. For two medium-sized flank steaks, about 1 cup should be enough. Save some dressing for a final drizzle and garnish. Add to the meat mixture chopped red bell pepper, lime zest and juice, essential oils, and salt and pepper to taste. Mix well. Let sit for at least an hour before plating.

For assembly I like to use pieces of butterleaf lettuce, hearts of romaine or endive leaves; however, flour or corn tortillas or miniature tostada shells work great. Garnish with a drizzle of dressing and a sprinkle of cotija or queso fresco cheese.

Cilantro Lime Rice

I like to make rice as a side dish. In a rice cooker, it is just as simple as set it and forget it. It keeps well in the refrigerator, making it a "cook once, eat twice" dish. It also feeds a lot of mouths, which is great when you have children or teenagers that eat a lot.

– Chef John

INGREDIENTS

1 1/2 CUP JASMINE OR LONG-GRAIN RICE, RINSED AND DRAINED TWICE

3 1/2 CUPS VEGETABLE BROTH OR WATER

1 TEASPOON GROUND TURMERIC

1/2 TEASPOON SALT

3/4 CUP FINELY CHOPPED CILANTRO, WASHED AND DRIED

1 TABLESPOON VEGETABLE OIL

2 TABLESPOONS BUTTER OR BUTTER SUBSTITUTE

3/4 CUP RED BELL PEPPER, VERY SMALL DICED

3/4 CUP YELLOW BELL PEPPER, VERY SMALL DICE

3/4 CUP GREEN BELL PEPPER, VERY SMALL DICE

1 CUP RED ONION, VERY SMALL DICE (ABOUT 1 SMALL RED ONION)

2 LIMES, ZESTED AND JUICED

10 DROPS OF LIME ESSENTIAL OIL

10 DROPS OF CILANTRO ESSENTIAL OIL

5 DROPS OF BLACK PEPPER ESSENTIAL OIL

DIRECTIONS

In rice cooker add rice, water, turmeric, and salt. Prepare according to machine directions. It will take about 20 minutes. (Makes 4 1/2 cups rice.)

While rice is cooking, heat a nonstick 3-quart saucepot over medium high heat. Add oil and wait for 5 seconds, then add butter, onions, and peppers. Sauté just until they just start to turn color, about 3-5 minutes. Remove from heat. Mix in the essential oils, juice and zest of two limes then set aside.

When rice is done, mix rice into pot of lime and onion pepper mix and fold in gently. You don't want to smash the rice. Add salt and pepper to taste.

I like this dish with the Thai Red Curry and Meatballs recipe in this book.

NOTE ABOUT CILANTRO

Cilantro is grown in sand and tends to be very dirty even after being "washed" at the store. Before using, wash or rinse it very well under running water. To dry it, roll the cilantro up in a hand towel or several layers of paper towels and squeeze. If you don't dry it well, the cilantro will turn into a soggy wet mess when you start chopping.

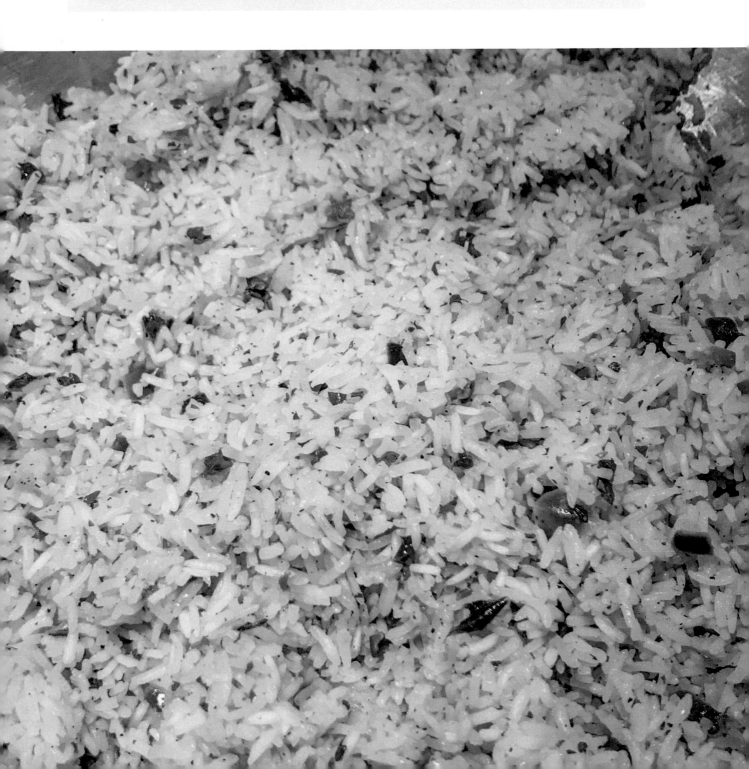

Cinnamon Orange French Toast

When we have leftover bread, a once-in-a-while special treat is to make French toast. Using the cinnamon and orange essential oils really wows the flavor. For the maple syrup, combine a pure Vermont maple syrup with a little bit of aged bourbon for a great flavor. Of course, this version is adults-only. The essential oils match the bourbon flavor nicely.

– Chef John

INGREDIENTS

4 SLICES DAY-OLD RUSTIC ITALIAN BREAD, CUT 3/4 INCH THICK

3 EGGS

1 CUP MILK OR MILK SUBSTITUTE

10 DROPS ORANGE ESSENTIAL OIL

3 DROPS CINNAMON BARK ESSENTIAL OIL

2 TEASPOONS GROUND CINNAMON

2 TEASPOONS VANILLA EXTRACT

2 TABLESPOONS BUTTER

1 TABLESPOON GHEE

CINNAMON-SUGAR SPRINKLE

POWDERED SUGAR

MAPLE SYRUP

DIRECTIONS

Melt butter and ghee in skillet over medium low heat. Mix eggs, milk, oils, cinnamon, and vanilla in bowl. Dip bread slices in egg mixture, then place in heated skillet. Sprinkle cinnamon sugar on the up-facing side of bread while cooking. When bottom is browned, turn over. Continue cooking until browned on both sides. Dust with powdered sugar. Serve with maple syrup for dipping. Makes 4 servings.

Cranberry Cider Cooler

I got inspired to create this drink by all of the sage in my garden and by cranberry season. I tried this Austin East Spiced Cider with it that was great. Add in Bacardi Gold Rum and BAM, there it is. The addition of the essential oils took it over the top. You will think you are drinking Thanksgiving with this drink.

– Chef John

CRANBERRY SAGE SIMPLE SYRUP

1 TABLESPOON FREEZE-DRIED CRANBERRIES, GROUND
1 CUP OF WATER
2 CUPS OF SUGAR
1 CAN WHOLE-BERRY CRANBERRY SAUCE

ONE LARGE SPRIG OF SAGE
5 DROPS ORANGE ESSENTIAL OIL
4 DROPS SAGE ESSENTIAL OIL

DIRECTIONS

In a medium saucepan bring to a boil the water, sugar, cranberry, and sage for three minutes, stirring once. Remove from heat, cover and set aside until room temperature. Pick out the sage. Drop in essential oils. If you plan to store this for later use, you may have to refresh the essential oils before using later, as they will dissipate over time.

Cranberry Cider Cooler

INGREDIENTS

4 OUNCES DRY CIDER BEER
2 OUNCES GOLD RUM
2 OUNCES OF CRANBERRY SAGE SIMPLE SYRUP (PREVIOUS PAGE)

DIRECTIONS

In a tall cocktail glass filled with ice, first pour in cider, then rum, then syrup. The cranberry will sink to the bottom, so drinking with a straw is nice. Garnish with fresh sage leaf.

Fennel Slaw

My wife and I often host multiple course chef's tasting charity dinners at our house. One dinner we had was themed completely vegan for all courses at the request of several of our vegan and vegetarian friends. I served the Twice Cooked Baked Polenta (recipe in this book) with this Fennel Slaw as the topping. The flavors of the two dishes meld well but also maintain separate identity.

— Chef John

INGREDIENTS

2 BULBS OF FRESH FENNEL (STALK AND FRONDS), SHAVED OR SLICED EXTREMELY THIN WITH CORE REMOVED

2 TABLESPOONS EXTRA VIRGIN OLIVE OIL

2 TEASPOONS RICE WINE VINEGAR

2 TEASPOONS LEMON JUICE

2 SPRIGS OF FRESH DILL, CHOPPED (ABOUT 1 TABLESPOON) (FREEZE DRIED DILL WORKS WELL FOR THIS IF YOU CAN'T GET FRESH)

5 DROPS FENNEL ESSENTIAL OIL

5 DROPS DILL ESSENTIAL OIL

3 DROPS BLACK PEPPER ESSENTIAL OIL

SALT AND PEPPER TO TASTE

DIRECTIONS

Preheat oven to 400 degrees. On an aluminum foil or parchment paper lined sheet pan, place fennel and oil in pan and cook in oven for about 15-20 minutes until it takes on a little color, but not roasted. Remove from pan and place in mixing bowl. Add the remaining ingredients and toss together. Add salt and pepper to taste. Let cool to room temperature or chill in the refrigerator. After it cools, add a 1 or 2 more drops of essential oils. If the fresh fennel is not in season, adding another drop of fennel essential oil will help bring back the true fennel flavor. These flavors are strong and bold, so add or take away to your liking.

Homemade Hummus

Hummus is a staple at our essential oil parties. It is a simple base dip that can be made into many different variations. I like to make homemade hummus because it is easy and fast. No need to buy the prepared varieties. I like knowing what I have put in my hummus. I use high quality oils and other ingredients, with no preservatives. When I add essential oils, I know I get the healthful properties as well. Hummus is great as a condiment on sandwiches or in pitas with chicken and veggies.

– Chef John

HUMMUS BASE

1 (24-OUNCE) CAN CANNELLINI BEANS, WASHED AND DRAINED
1 LEMON, JUICED
3 GARLIC CLOVES, CHOPPED

1/2 CUP TAHINI PASTE
SALT AND PEPPER
1/4 CUP EXTRA-VIRGIN OLIVE OIL

DIRECTIONS

Add all ingredients in a food processor, reserving the 1/2 cup of olive oil. Blend until creamy. At this point, you can add any of the variations below.

Simple Hummus

INGREDIENTS

2 CUPS HUMMUS BASE (ABOVE)
1/2 OLIVE OIL
1 TABLESPOON WATER

DIRECTIONS

If you want Simple Hummus, then add the additional 1/2 cup oil and add one tablespoon of water slowly until it resembles the consistency of cake frosting.

Roasted Pepper Basil Hummus

INGREDIENTS

2 CUPS HUMMUS BASE (ABOVE)
1 SMALL JAR ROASTED BELL PEPPERS, DRAINED AND DRIED
2 TEASPOONS FRESH CRACKED BLACK PEPPER
1/4 CUP FRESH BASIL, CHOPPED

JUICE OF ONE LEMON
6 DROPS LEMON ESSENTIAL OIL
12 DROPS BLACK PEPPER ESSENTIAL OIL
4 DROPS BASIL ESSENTIAL OIL

DIRECTIONS

Mix hummus, peppers, lemon juice, and essential oils together in food processor and blend until smooth and creamy. Top with cracked black pepper. Serve with pita chips or fresh cut veggies.

Lemon Pepper Hummus

INGREDIENTS

2 CUPS HUMMUS BASE (ABOVE)
2 TABLESPOONS OLIVE OIL
2 TEASPOON FRESH CRACKED BLACK PEPPER

10 DROPS LEMON ESSENTIAL OIL
5 DROPS BLACK PEPPER ESSENTIAL OIL
ZEST OF ONE LEMON

DIRECTIONS

Mix hummus, olive oil, and essential oils together. Top with cracked black pepper. Serve with pita chips. This hummus also is great with grilled veggies and spicy grilled chicken.

Lavender Flower Lemonade

I just love making lavender lemonade. It is quick and refreshing. I use dried lavender buds that you can get in the bulk section of the grocery store. The lavender buds add a nice pink color to the drink. Combining the lavender herbs and the lavender essential oil gives a depth of flavor that either alone could not provide.

– Chef John

LAVENDER TEA BASE

1/2 CUP OF DRIED LAVENDER BUDS
1 CUP WATER
3 DROPS LAVENDER ESSENTIAL OIL

DIRECTIONS

Heat water to just under boiling. Add lavender buds. Stir and steep for 3-5 minutes. Strain and set liquid aside to cool. After cooled, add essential oil.

LEMONADE BASE

3 CUPS FRESH LEMON JUICE
2 – 2 1/2 CUPS SPLENDA
5 DROPS LEMON ESSENTIAL OIL

DIRECTIONS

Mix lemon juice and Splenda until dissolved.

Lavender Flower Lemonade

INGREDIENTS

LAVENDER TEA BASE (ABOVE)
LEMONADE BASE (ABOVE)
WATER

DIRECTIONS

Mix lavender base and lemonade base into a gallon container. Add enough water to fill container. Stir. Makes one gallon.

Peppermint Patricia Brownies

See what I did with that name? Ha! These brownies are very strong in peppermint flavor. I like them that way. If you think they are too strong, just reduce the amount of peppermint essential oil. I also like to substitute the orange essential oil instead because I prefer chocolate and orange to peppermint. That variation is at the end of this recipe. These brownies are a staple at all of our oil parties!

– Chef John

INGREDIENTS

4 LARGE EGGS

1 1/4 CUPS GOOD DARK COCOA POWDER

1 1/2 TEASPOON SALT

1 TEASPOON BAKING POWDER

2 TABLESPOONS VANILLA EXTRACT

1 CUP UNSALTED BUTTER, SLIGHTLY SOFTENED, CUT INTO

ABOUT 16 PIECES

2 1/4 CUPS SUGAR

1 1/2 CUPS ALL-PURPOSE FLOUR

1 CUP MILK CHOCOLATE CHIPS

1 CUP DARK CHOCOLATE CHIPS

15 DROPS PEPPERMINT ESSENTIAL OIL

DIRECTIONS

Preheat oven to 350 degrees. Lightly grease or spray a 9x13 pan. In a large mixing bowl, combine the eggs, cocoa, salt, baking powder, and vanilla. Beat until smooth and silky. Set aside.

In a nonstick saucepan over low heat, combine the sugar and butter. Cook while stirring just until the mixture is hot, but not bubbling. It should start to have a nice shine.

Very quickly, combine both bowls and mix until smooth and creamy. A stand mixer or a hand mixer work well for this application.

Add the flour, chocolate chips and essential oils, stirring until smooth (2-3 minutes). If you want chunks of chocolate and don't want your chocolate chips to melt, let the mixture cool off for about 20 minutes before adding in the chocolate chips.

Pour the batter into greased pan and bake for about 30-35 minutes or until the edges of the brownies are crispy and firm. A toothpick inserted in the center should yield a little brownie residue while mostly clean. If you wait until the toothpick comes out totally clean they will be dry and overcooked. I always check at 25 minutes and every 5 min thereafter.

ORANGE BROWNIES

You can substitute 20 drops of orange essential oil instead of the peppermint essential oil. Orange has great synergy when used in combination with chocolate. Orange essential oil is not as dense as peppermint essential oil, so you will have to use a little more of it.

Pico de Gallo

My mother-in-law loved pico de gallo. She would eat it every day with tortilla chips. I wish she could have tried this version using essential oils. When you are preparing the jalapeno or serrano pepper, be sure to use gloves to remove the seeds and ribbing. I learned this from experience, believe me! One time of getting the peppers on your hands then touching your eyes, you won't soon forget to wear gloves!

– Chef John

INGREDIENTS

4 ROMA TOMATOES, DICED ABOUT A HALF INCH

1/2 CUP OR 1 SMALL YELLOW ONION, SMALL DICED

1/2 JALAPENO OR 1 WHOLE SERRANO, FINELY MINCED (FOR LESS HEAT REMOVE THE SEEDS AND THE WHITE RIB FROM THE INSIDE OF THE PEPPER)

2 CLOVES GARLIC, CRUSHED OR FINELY MINCED

2 TABLESPOONS FRESH LIME JUICE

1 TEASPOON FRESH GROUND BLACK PEPPER

10 DROPS CILANTRO ESSENTIAL OIL

3 DROPS OREGANO ESSENTIAL OIL

2 DROPS LIME ESSENTIAL OIL

SALT TO TASTE

DIRECTIONS

Place all ingredients into bowl. Mix well. Add salt to taste. Cover and refrigerate for at least an hour before using. Will keep up to 3 days in the refrigerator.

Pinto Bean Hummus

In Texas, we mash pinto beans and call it bean dip. That's been available in a can for a long time, but no one thought to call it hummus. Hummus is a bean purée usually made from chickpeas or white beans. We've been doing that a long time in Texas! I like to put it in half-pint jars because it's like opening a can of bean dip. Serve with corn chips. I love it!

– Chef John

INGREDIENTS

2 JALAPENOS, SEEDED, STEMMED, AND CUT IN HALF LENGTHWISE

1/2 MEDIUM ONION, QUARTERED

1 CLOVE GARLIC, PEELED

1/4 CUP WHITE VINEGAR

1/2 CUP WATER

2 TEASPOONS SALT

1/4 TEASPOON GROUND CUMIN

3 CUPS COOKED PINTO BEANS (OR 2 15-OUNCE CANS PINTO BEANS, DRAIN AND RESERVE LIQUID)

3/4 CUP RESERVED BEAN JUICE

2 TABLESPOONS CHILI POWDER

1 TABLESPOON PAPRIKA

1/4 TEASPOON CAYENNE (OR SUBSTITUTE MILD CHILI POWDER IF TOO HOT)

1 TABLESPOON BACON GREASE (OR SUBSTITUTE VEGETABLE OIL OR MELTED UNSALTED BUTTER)

4 OUNCES GRATED MONTERREY JACK CHEESE

5 DROPS BLACK PEPPER ESSENTIAL OIL

2 DROPS CILANTRO ESSENTIAL OIL

2 DROPS CUMIN ESSENTIAL OIL

DIRECTIONS

Place jalapenos, onion, garlic, vinegar, water, salt, and cumin in pot. Cover with water. Bring to boil. Turn off heat, cover, and let steep for 10 minutes. With slotted spoon, transfer jalapenos, onion, garlic, and 1 tablespoon of liquid to food processor. Add beans, bean juice, chili powder, paprika, and cayenne. Blend until smooth and creamy.

On low-medium heat, melt the bacon grease in a skillet and add the bean purée. Cook for 5 minutes, stirring occasionally until slightly thickened and fragrant. Stir in cheese until just melted. Add essential oils. Taste and add salt if needed to preference. Serve either warm or chilled with corn chips.

Pumpkin Soup with Pepitas

I have several family members that have pretty significant food sensitivities. I like to make this particular pumpkin soup dairy free and gluten-free. Believe it or not, even though it is lighter and thinner than the traditional pumpkin bisque, by no means does it lack flavor.

– Chef John

INGREDIENTS

1 2-3 POUND SMALL PIE PUMPKIN, ROASTED AND PEELED

2 MEDIUM YUKON GOLD POTATOES, PEELED AND CUT IN QUARTERS

2 CUPS CHICKEN BROTH OR VEGETABLE STOCK

1/4 TEASPOON SALT

1/4 TEASPOON GROUND GINGER

1/4 TEASPOON GROUND CINNAMON

1/4 TEASPOON GROUND NUTMEG

1 PINCH BLACK PEPPER

12 OUNCES UNSWEETENED, UNFLAVORED, NON-DAIRY MILK SUBSTITUTE

3 DROPS CARDAMOM ESSENTIAL OIL

2 DROPS NUTMEG ESSENTIAL OIL

1 DROP CINNAMON BARK ESSENTIAL OIL

DIRECTIONS

In a medium saucepan, combine pumpkin, potato, chicken broth, salt, spices. Bring to a boil and reduce heat to a simmer. Stir every 3-4 minutes with a silicone spatula for 20 minutes or until potatoes are tender. Turn off of heat and puree with an immersion blender, adding the evaporated milk into the mixture while blending. Blend until smooth. Let cool to warm then add essential oils. Season last with salt and pepper to taste. Garnish each serving with a sprinkle of toasted pumpkin seeds and a drizzle of a good Balsamic reduction.

Pumpkin Spice Latte

Who can miss the famous coffee place that brings out the pumpkin every fall? Well, I decided, why spend all that money going out for pumpkin when I can make it at my house, the way I like it, and know what ingredients are in it? No chemicals or preservatives. I can add the sweetener of my choice and you can add your preference. Then I can add oils to pump the health-supporting properties. Much better!

– Chef John

PUMPKIN SPICE ESSENTIAL OIL BLEND

4 DROPS CINNAMON BARK ESSENTIAL OIL

2 DROPS GINGER ESSENTIAL OIL

2 DROPS CLOVE ESSENTIAL OIL

4 DROPS CARDAMOM ESSENTIAL OIL

4 DROPS NUTMEG ESSENTIAL OIL

3 ML MCT LIQUID UNFLAVORED OIL.

DIRECTIONS

Combine all ingredients and put in clean essential oil bottle with dropper cap on.

LATTE MIXER

1 CUP MILK OR MILK SUBSTITUTE

1/4 CUP CANNED PUMPKIN PUREE

3 PACKETS SPLENDA OR ANY NON-SUGAR SWEETENER OF YOUR CHOICE

1/2 TEASPOON VANILLA

20 DROPS PUMPKIN SPICE ESSENTIAL OIL BLEND (ABOVE)

1 TEASPOON DRIED PUMPKIN PIE SPICE

DIRECTIONS

Combine all ingredients. Refrigerate and let sit for about an hour before using. Store in the refrigerator in a Mason jar. Shake well before each use. This will last about 4-5 days if using milk or 10 days if using a milk substitute.

Pumpkin Spice Latte

INGREDIENTS

1/2 CUP PUMPKIN SPICE LATTE MIXER (ABOVE)
1/4 CUP MILK OR MILK SUBSTITUTE
DOUBLE SHOT OF ESPRESSO

ALTERNATIVE: 2 OUNCES COLD BREW COFFEE OR 1/4 CUP
STRONG COFFEE

DIRECTIONS

Pour Pumpkin Spice Latte Mixer and milk in microwave safe cup and microwave on high for 1 minute, stirring after 30 seconds. Remove and add espresso then heat slightly in microwave until desired temperature is reached. Makes one drink.

Pumpkin Spice Latte Protein Shake

INGREDIENTS

1 CUP CRUSHED ICE
1 SCOOP MCT POWDER
2 SCOOPS VANILLA PROTEIN POWDER
2 SHOTS ESPRESSO OR 2 OUNCES COLD BREW COFFEE

CONCENTRATE
4 OZ PUMPKIN SPICE LATTE MIXER
4 OZ MILK OR ANY MILK SUBSTITUTE

DIRECTIONS

Blend all ingredients on high until smooth. Add a little more liquid to get your desired consistency. Makes one drink.

Quinoa Tabbouleh

Quinoa is pretty much the perfect food! It contains all 23 amino acids, including the 9 essential amino acids that make a complete protein, and is a good source of protein for vegan and vegetarian types. This recipe is vegan and vegetarian-friendly. Quinoa is a good substitute for rice if you are counting carbs. It is still a grain, but a whole grain and much healthier overall than plain white rice. The herbs and oils make this dish very light, great for a hot summer day!

– Chef John

INGREDIENTS

1 CUP QUINOA, RINSED WELL

1/2 TEASPOON KOSHER SALT

2 TABLESPOONS FRESH LEMON JUICE

1 CLOVE GARLIC, MINCED

1/2 CUP EXTRA VIRGIN OLIVE OIL

1/2 TEASPOON GROUND BLACK PEPPER

1 PINT CHERRY TOMATOES, HALVED

1 LARGE ENGLISH HOTHOUSE CUCUMBER OR 2 PERSIAN CUCUMBERS, CUT INTO 1/4 INCH PIECES

2/3 CUP FLAT-LEAF PARSLEY, CHOPPED

1/2 CUP FRESH MINT LEAVES, CHOPPED

2 SCALLIONS, THINLY SLICED

2 DROPS PEPPERMINT ESSENTIAL OIL

4 DROPS LEMON ESSENTIAL OIL

DIRECTIONS

Bring quinoa, 1/2 teaspoon salt, and 1 1/4 cups water to a boil in a medium saucepan over high heat. Reduce heat to medium-low, cover, and simmer until quinoa is tender, about 10 minutes. Remove from heat and let stand, covered, for 5 minutes. Fluff with a fork.

Meanwhile, whisk lemon juice and garlic in a small bowl. Gradually whisk in olive oil. Add essential oils. Season dressing to taste with salt and pepper.

Spread out quinoa on a large rimmed baking sheet; let cool. Transfer to a large bowl; mix in 1/4 cup dressing. Add cucumber, tomatoes, herbs, and scallions to bowl with quinoa; toss to coat. Season to taste with salt and pepper. Drizzle remaining dressing over.

This can be made a day in advance. Just store the dressing and quinoa separately, then mix when ready to serve.

Rainbow Carrots with Lemon and Thyme

Promise me that you are not buying those little misshapen orange sort-of carrots! Did you know that "real" carrots come in many colors, not just orange? Go find some at a grocery store with a good produce section. They are so yummy and healthy too. The nutrients in the colors are so much better for you. I never peel my carrots either. Just wash them. There's nutrients in the peel, so don't take that off.

– Chef John

INGREDIENTS

2 POUNDS LARGE RAINBOW CARROTS (RED, WHITE, ORANGE AND PURPLE COLORS;)

4 TABLESPOONS EXTRA VIRGIN OLIVE OIL

1 CUP VEGETABLE STOCK

2 TABLESPOONS HONEY

2 CLOVES GARLIC, SMASHED

2 SPRIGS FRESH THYME

2 TABLESPOONS UNSALTED BUTTER

3 DROPS THYME ESSENTIAL OIL

4 DROPS LEMON ESSENTIAL OIL

PINCH OF SALT

1/2 TEASPOON FRESH GROUND BLACK PEPPER

DIRECTIONS

Preheat oven to 400 degrees. Add unpeeled carrots, olive oil, vegetable stock, garlic, thyme, sugar, salt, and pepper to a shallow baking dish. Cover and roast in oven for 45 minutes to 1 hour or until carrots are fork tender; remove and let chill in refrigerator for about 30 minutes. Reserve liquid. In a small saucepot, heat liquid slowly and reduce to a syrupy glaze. Remove from heat. Add butter and stir until it is melted and incorporated. Stir in essential oils and set aside. Place on foil-lined baking sheet. Brush carrots with the syrup mixture and heat in oven at 400 degrees for about 15 minutes before serving.

Romanoff's Strawberries

I did a cooking demo where I had no heat source. I could only do a cold preparation. This dish was a superb hit! The essential oils in the cream really make this dish stand out from all other variations out there. The freeze-dried strawberries add a great extra depth and dimension of intense natural, strawberry flavor.

— Chef John

MARINATED STRAWBERRIES

2 PINTS STRAWBERRIES, CUT IN HALF WITH STEMS REMOVED

2 OUNCES FREEZE-DRIED STRAWBERRIES, CRUSHED

2 TABLESPOONS GRANULATED SUGAR

1 OZ FAVORITE VODKA (OR SUBSTITUTE 1 ADDITIONAL TEASPOON SUGAR AND 1 OUNCE OF WATER)

4 DROPS ORANGE ESSENTIAL OIL

2 DROPS BLACK PEPPER ESSENTIAL OIL

DIRECTIONS

Add all ingredients to a mixing bowl and mix well. Marinate strawberries in refrigerator for about a half hour.

MASCARPONE CREAM

8-OUNCE PACKAGE MASCARPONE CHEESE

4 OUNCES SOUR CREAM

1 TABLESPOON VANILLA

2 TABLESPOONS GRANULATED SUGAR

1 HEAPING SPOONFUL OF FREEZE-DRIED STRAWBERRIES

DIRECTIONS

In medium size mixing bowl, mix mascarpone cheese until smooth and creamy, about 30 seconds. Add sour cream, sugar, vanilla, freeze-dried strawberries. Mix together with mixer for an additional 30 seconds, until it is all incorporated. Set aside in refrigerator until ready to serve.

Romanoff's Strawberries

DIRECTIONS

To serve, divide strawberry cream mixture into 4 chilled dessert bowls. Top each with a portion of the marinated strawberries.

Traditionally, this dish had no pastry or cookies. The "American style" of the dish is often seen with a shortbread cookie crushed on top as garnish for texture.

Swedish Meatballs

My mother's family originated in Sweden. Many of our traditional family recipes are Swedish in nature – the Swedish flavors and recipes were passed down through the family. This dish was a comfort food for us when I was growing up. Warm in your tummy and substantial – it takes me back to when I was a kid.

– Chef John

MEATBALLS

2 1/2 POUNDS GROUND PORK

1 POUND LEAN GROUND BEEF

2 LARGE EGGS, LIGHTLY BEATEN

1/2 CUP MILK

4 SLICES GOOD QUALITY WHITE BREAD, CRUSTS REMOVED AND ROUGHLY TORN INTO BITE-SIZED PIECES

4 CLOVES GARLIC, MINCED

1/4 CUP GRATED PARMESAN

3/4 CUP RICOTTA

1/4 TEASPOON DRIED CHILE FLAKES

1/4 TEASPOON FENNEL SEEDS

ZEST OF 1 LEMON, FINELY GRATED

30 DROPS BLACK PEPPER ESSENTIAL OIL

20 DROPS FENNEL ESSENTIAL OIL

20 DROPS CORIANDER ESSENTIAL OIL

SALT AND PEPPER TO TASTE

1/2 CUP OLIVE OIL

DIRECTIONS

To make the meatballs, place ground meats in a large bowl and stir in eggs. Put the milk and the bread into a food processor. Let the bread soak for a minute while you add garlic, parmesan, ricotta, chile flakes, fennel seeds, and zest of lemon. Pulse everything until the mixture is just combined. Add essential oils to bread mix. Then, add to the meat and mix well. Use small ice cream scoop to form meatballs and chill in the fridge until ready to use.

When ready, preheat oven to 350 degrees. Heat half of oil in a frying pan. Add about half the meatballs at a time and fry over medium heat for 10 minutes, turning frequently, until golden brown. Remove them from the pan with slotted spoon and transfer them to an ovenproof dish. Bake this pan of meatballs for another 5 minutes while you finish cooking the rest of the meatballs. Add oil to the pan and fry remaining meatballs, then place in oven for 5 minutes. When all meatballs are finished, set aside.

If you want to save these for another day, place in a resealable plastic bag and cool completely in refrigerator. Then, freeze the extra meatballs for up to 2 weeks for a quick and easy dinner.

NOTE ABOUT THE FRENCH SPOON TECHNIQUE

To test how ready your sauce is, dip a wood or metal spoon into the sauce mixture. Turn it over to see the back of the spoon. Run your finger through the middle of the sauce. If the swiped area stays cleanly separated, the sauce is ready.

SWEDISH MEATBALL SAUCE

3 1/2 OUNCES BUTTER, DIVIDED

1/3 CUP PLAIN FLOUR

3 CUPS GOOD QUALITY BEEF STOCK

1/4 CUP FENNEL FRONDS, FINELY CHOPPED

1/2 TEASPOON GROUND NUTMEG

1/2 TEASPOON ALLSPICE

10 OUNCES SOUR CREAM

2/3 CUP FRESHLY GRATED PARMESAN

1 1/4 CUPS CHERRY JAM, DIVIDED

5 DROPS NUTMEG ESSENTIAL OIL

5 DROPS FENNEL ESSENTIAL OIL

1 DROP CLOVE ESSENTIAL OIL

SALT AND FRESH GROUND PEPPER TO TASTE

COOKED WIDE EGG NOODLES

ADDITIONAL FENNEL FRONDS FOR GARNISH

DIRECTIONS

Place sauté pan on burner on medium low heat and add butter to melt. Once melted, wait about a minute more. It should be hot enough that when you add a pinch of flour it will slowly start to bubble. Using a silicone spatula or a wooden spoon, add all of the flour and stir, scraping the brown bits off the bottom as you go. After stirring for about two minutes constantly, it should resemble wet sand. Add stock along with the herbs, spices, essential oils, a small pinch of salt and whisk to combine. Stir sauce until it thickens, about 8-10 minutes.

Remove from heat. Add sour cream, Parmesan, fennel fronds, and 1/4 cup cherry jam. Whisk together and simmer for 3-5 minutes, until velvety smooth and thick enough to coat the back of a spoon. Season to taste with salt and pepper.

SWEDISH MEATBALLS

If your pan is ovenproof, you can place meatballs into the sauce and place directly in the oven. Or, transfer sauce and meatballs to an ovenproof dish and place in the oven for 10-12 min.

Serve meatballs and sauce garnished with the fresh fennel fronds over cooked wide egg noodles. Serve remaining cherry jam on the side.

Thai Cashew Chicken Salad in Wonton Cups

I created this recipe for an essential oils party we had recently. I liked the idea of making small bites in wonton cups. Thai flavors meld well with the available essential oils, too. This was a huge hit. Friends from that party have asked me for the recipe. When I create a new recipe, I don't really write it down at the time I make it. It's more about the artistry in that moment. So, now I have finally recorded the recipe for you here.

– Chef John

THAI CASHEW DRESSING

16 OUNCES CASHEW BUTTER

1/4 CUP TOASTED SESAME OIL

1/4 CUP ASIAN SWEET RED CHILI SAUCE

1/4 CUP RICE WINE VINEGAR

1/4 CUP MAPLE SYRUP

2 TABLESPOONS GROUND GINGER

2 TABLESPOONS GROUND LEMONGRASS

1 TEASPOON SALT

15 DROPS LEMONGRASS ESSENTIAL OIL

1 DROP CORIANDER ESSENTIAL OIL

4 DROPS CILANTRO ESSENTIAL OIL

5 DROPS CARDAMOM ESSENTIAL OIL

DIRECTIONS

Add all ingredients to food processor and pulse about 6 times. Scrape sides down with rubber spatula and repeat 2 more times. If too thick, add about 1/4 cup water while food processor is running until a smooth consistency is reached. Taste and adjust seasonings as needed. Place in sealed container in the refrigerator for about an hour. Let sit out for 10-15 minutes before serving to soften.

These can be made up to a week ahead of time or frozen for 2-3 months in a sealed container.

CASHEW CHICKEN SALAD

2 CUPS COOKED DICED CHICKEN (SEE OPTIONS BELOW)

3 CUPS WATER

3 TABLESPOONS SALT

1 CUP CASHEWS, COARSELY CHOPPED

3/4 CUP RED ONION, VERY FINELY CHOPPED (ABOUT 1 SMALL OR 1/2 OF A LARGE ONION)

3/4 CUP CELERY, VERY FINELY CHOPPED (ABOUT 2 STALKS)

1 CUP BELL PEPPER, DICED

1 CUP + 2 TABLESPOONS THAI CASHEW DRESSING (PREVIOUS PAGE)

1/2 CUP GREEN ONIONS (GREEN AND WHITE PARTS), THINLY SLICED

1/2 CUP CILANTRO, FINELY CHOPPED

BLACK SESAME SEEDS FOR GARNISH

SALT AND BLACK PEPPER TO TASTE

PACKAGE WONTON WRAPPERS

DIRECTIONS

Preheat oven to 350 degrees. Spray a miniature muffin pan with cooking spray. Lay each wonton wrapper into the cup of a muffin pan, pressing down the edges to form small cups with flat bottoms. Bake 5-7 minutes until golden. Immediately remove and cool.

In a medium saucepot, add salt to water and bring to a boil. Add chopped cashews and boil for 10 minutes, then drain. In a small bowl, toss cashews with 2 tablespoons of Thai Cashew Dressing, then refrigerate to cool for at least 30 minutes.

In a medium size mixing bowl, add all remaining ingredients and mix well. If it seems too thick, then add a little more dressing as desired. Refrigerate for an hour for flavors to blend.

To serve, place 1 heaping tablespoon of chicken mixture into wonton cups and garnish with a sprinkle of black sesame seeds and thinly sliced green onions. I like to use both for the depth of color in presentation.

These can be made and refrigerated up to three hours ahead without sacrificing the texture of the wonton cups. The chicken mixture can be made ahead and placed in sealed container or sealable sandwich bag for up to 3 days ahead of serving. If you are going to make the mixture ahead of time, wait to make the wonton cups fresh, as they are better when served shortly ahead of serving.

Options: Leftover turkey or grilled steak work great as well. If you use breast meat instead of thigh or dark meat, you might have to add more dressing so it will not be too dry.

Thai Red Curry with Lemongrass Meatballs

My wife thinks she doesn't like Thai food until I make it at home. After her weight-loss surgery, we ate a lot of ground meats because they were easier to digest. These lemongrass and ginger meatballs have unexpected flavor from a traditional Italian or Swedish meatball. The recipe as written calls for ground beef. Understand that when I buy ground beef, I usually buy organic, grass-fed and grass-finished. I believe that you should buy the best quality ingredients you can afford and simply eat less of them. You can also substitute ground turkey or chicken in this recipe for the beef, if you prefer. However, if you do that, I strongly recommend using dark meat so the meatballs are not too dry.

— Chef John

THAI RED CURRY SAUCE

1/4 CUP COCONUT OIL OR OLIVE OIL

1 LARGE YELLOW ONION, CHOPPED (ABOUT 1 1/2 CUPS)

1 LARGE RED ONION, CUT IN HALF AND SLICED INTO 1/4 INCH STRIPS (ABOUT 1 1/2 CUPS)

2 TABLESPOONS FINELY GRATED FRESH GINGER (ABOUT A 2-INCH NUB OF GINGER ABOUT THE SIZE OF YOUR THUMB), DIVIDED IN HALF

3 CLOVES GARLIC, CRUSHED

3 CLOVES GARLIC, SLICED THIN

1 EACH RED AND GREEN BELL PEPPERS, SLICED INTO THIN 1/2 INCH X 2-INCH LONG STRIPS

2 CARROTS, PEELED CUT IN HALF AND SLICED ABOUT 1/4 INCH THICK (ABOUT 1 CUP)

2 TABLESPOONS THAI RED CURRY PASTE

2 CUPS VEGETABLE BROTH

2 CANS (14 OUNCES) REGULAR FULL FAT COCONUT MILK

1 TABLESPOON TAMARI

2 TEASPOONS FRESH LIME JUICE

5 DROPS LIME ESSENTIAL OIL

3 DROPS GINGER ESSENTIAL OIL

4 DROPS BASIL ESSENTIAL OIL

1/4 TEASPOON SALT (MORE TO TASTE)

GARNISHES/SIDES: HANDFUL OF CHOPPED FRESH BASIL OR CILANTRO

Thai Red Curry
with Lemongrass Meatballs

DIRECTIONS

Heat a large skillet with deep sides on medium high over medium heat. Once it is very hot, add the oil, carrots, onion and a pinch of salt and sauté, stirring often, until the onion has softened and is turning translucent, about 5 minutes.

Add the ginger and garlic and cook just until fragrant, about 30 seconds, while stirring continuously.

Immediately add the bell peppers and cook 3-5 more minutes, stirring occasionally. Dissolve the curry pasted into the vegetable stock and add to skillet. Cook for about 2 minutes continually, stirring slowly. Bring to a simmer.

Add the coconut milk and stir to combine while the mixture simmers slightly over medium/low heat for about 20-30 minutes. Stir often so as not to burn or stick to the bottom of the pan.

Remove the pot from the heat and season with tamari and lime juice. Add salt to taste. If the curry needs a little more rounded flavor, add 1/2 teaspoon more tamari. For greater acidity, add 1/2 teaspoon of additional rice vinegar or lime juice.

Thai Red Curry with Lemongrass Meatballs

LEMONGRASS MEATBALLS

4 POUNDS VERY LEAN GROUND BEEF

2 OUNCES FRESH GINGER, MINCED

2 OUNCES FRESH LEMONGRASS, FINELY CHOPPED

2 OUNCES GARLIC, MINCED

15 DROPS LEMONGRASS ESSENTIAL OIL

15 DROPS BAY LAUREL ESSENTIAL OIL

3 TABLESPOONS SALT

4 TABLESPOONS BLACK PEPPER

1 TABLESPOON WHITE PEPPER

1 QUART VEGETABLE OIL

DIRECTIONS

Heat vegetable oil in a deep pot heated to 400 degrees. I use a high temperature candy thermometer for temperature regulation.

Mix all ingredients in a very large mixing bowl. Squish all together—I use my hands—for at least 2-3 minutes. Cover with plastic wrap and refrigerate for at least an hour to let the flavors absorb and blend.

Spray two cookie sheets with nonstick spray. Using a small ice cream scoop, form meatballs and place on cookie sheet. Place 10-12 (no more than that) into the heated oil for frying. Adding too many will drop the oil temperature too much and they will absorb the oil versus creating a crispy outer crust. When brown, lift out of oil with a slotted spoon and drain on paper towels or on a paper bag.

You can freeze the leftovers and they will keep for at least a month. If you use a vacuum sealer, the meatballs will keep for 4-6 months. I usually double the batch when good grass-fed beef is on sale and freeze in a vacuum sealer.

To serve: Divide meatballs evenly into 5 or 6 bowls ladle curry sauce on top. Garnish with chopped cilantro or fresh torn basil leaves.

You can serve the meatballs and sauce over plain jasmine rice. I also like the Cilantro Lime Rice recipe in this book with the Thai Red Curry dish.

Three-Bean Vegetarian Chili with Cilantro Cream

When I worked as a culinary instructor, my students entered a chili cook-off for a festival in Plano, Texas cooking contest against other culinary school and made this recipe. We won a first-place trophy in that contest! My Texas friends may try to say that Texas chili doesn't have beans in it. They are right, but this is not Texas chili. In fact, there are many regional and societal variations on chili. It is a vegan and vegetarian-friendly chili. Even still, meat eaters will enjoy this flavorful chili for a meatless Monday night dinner on a cold winter evening. Serve it with a little cornbread, and they will never miss the meat.

– Chef John

THREE-BEAN VEGETARIAN CHILI

2 TABLESPOONS OLIVE OIL

2 CUPS ONION, SMALL DICED

2 CUPS GREEN PEPPERS, SMALL DICED

2 CUPS CELERY, SMALL DICED

2 TABLESPOONS FINELY CHOPPED GARLIC

4 TABLESPOONS FINELY CHOPPED JALAPENO PEPPERS

4 TABLESPOONS DARK CHILI POWDER

1 TABLESPOON GROUND CUMIN

3 TABLESPOONS FRESH GROUND BLACK PEPPER

2 TEASPOONS DRIED MEXICAN OREGANO

1 TEASPOON GROUND CLOVES

1 16-OUNCE CAN PINTO BEANS, DRAINED

1 16-OUNCE CAN KIDNEY BEANS, DRAINED

1 16-OUNCE CAN BLACK BEANS, DRAINED

1 28-OUNCE CAN DICED TOMATOES WITH JUICE

3 CUPS VEGETABLE BROTH (TASTES BETTER THAN WATER BUT WATER IS FINE)

2 DROPS OREGANO ESSENTIAL OIL

10 DROPS BLACK PEPPER ESSENTIAL OIL

10 DROPS CARDAMOM ESSENTIAL OIL

CILANTRO CREAM FOR GARNISH (RECIPE BELOW)

DIRECTIONS

In large heavy saucepan, heat oil over medium heat; then add onions, bell pepper, celery, garlic, jalapenos and chili powder. Sweat vegetables, stirring occasionally, until softened, about 10 minutes. Do not overcook.

Add cumin, oregano, and cloves; cook for 1 minute until fragrant. Add beans, tomatoes and vegetable broth; stir to combine. Turn heat up to high and bring just up to a boil, then reduce heat to a simmer. Cover and cook about 30 minutes, stirring occasionally.

Uncover pot and cook over medium low heat, stirring occasionally, until beans begin falling apart and chili has achieved desired consistency (about 15 minutes). If it is too thick, add a little water or vegetable broth to thin it out. Season to taste.

Garnish with Cilantro Cream (recipe below). My wife and son love to serve this with crushed corn chips on top.

CILANTRO CREAM

1 LARGE BUNCH CILANTRO, RINSED, DRIED AND FINELY CHOPPED BY HAND

1/2 CUP MILK (OR MILK SUBSTITUTE)

1 24-OUNCE CONTAINER OF SOUR CREAM

1 TEASPOON LIME JUICE (ABOUT HALF A LIME)

10 DROPS CILANTRO ESSENTIAL OIL

10 DROPS LIME ESSENTIAL OIL

1/2 TEASPOON SALT

1 TEASPOON GROUND BLACK PEPPER

DIRECTIONS

Place cilantro and milk in blender. Purée on high for 15-30 seconds or until smooth and no large pieces of cilantro remain. Set aside.

In a medium size mixing bowl, whisk sour cream until smooth and creamy. Add cilantro milk and remaining ingredients and mix well. Add salt and pepper to taste.

Twice-Cooked Baked Polenta

Polenta is not so much an ingredient as it is actually a dish from northern Italy. We think of polenta nowadays as a form of Italian "grits." Even though grits and polenta are not exactly the same, they are cooked in much the same way. Both are slow-cooked in liquid until the grains swell and the starches are released. It will have a thick, creamy consistency. At this point in the process almost anything can be added to enhance richness or flavor, like a splash of cream, butter or cheese, and the dish is ready to be eaten. After is has cooled or been chilled, the consistency changes and it solidifies extremely firm. In this cooled solid form, it can be cut into pieces and crisped up on the outside by frying, baking, or grilling.

– Chef John

INGREDIENTS

VEGETABLE OIL SPRAY

6 CUPS CHICKEN OR VEGETABLE STOCK (OR WATER)

2 CUPS INSTANT POLENTA

1 TABLESPOON SALT

1/2 CUP + 1/3 CUP FINELY GRATED PARMESAN OR AGED MANCHEGO (OPTION FOR VEGANS, LEAVE THIS OUT)

3 TABLESPOONS + 3 TABLESPOONS WHOLE BUTTER (OR BUTTER SUBSTITUTE)

1/2 CUP CHOPPED BASIL LEAVES (PREFERABLY PURPLE BASIL IF YOU CAN FIND IT)

1 16-OUNCE JAR ROASTED RED BELL PEPPERS DRAINED, DRIED WELL, AND MEDIUM DICED

5 DROPS LEMON ESSENTIAL OIL

5 DROPS BAY LAUREL ESSENTIAL OIL

3 DROPS SAGE ESSENTIAL OIL

4 TABLESPOONS OLIVE OIL

FRESH GROUND BLACK PEPPER

Polenta

DIRECTIONS

Generously spray a 9x13 baking dish and set aside-one with deep square sides works best. Over medium-high heat bring to the boil the stock, 3 tablespoons of the butter, salt and roasted peppers. Gradually add the polenta in a thin steady stream, whisking constantly, until combined. Reduce heat to medium and cook, stirring continuously and scraping off of the bottom with a heat resistant silicone spatula, for 2 minutes or until the mixture thickens and the polenta is soft. A silicone spatula makes it much easier to scrape the sides down and off of the bottom to prevent burning and overcooking.

Remove from heat and stir in the parmesan and the remaining 3 tablespoons of the butter. Pour the mixture into the greased pan spray a light coating of vegetable spray on top and smooth the surface with the spatula until it is smooth and even. Set aside for 30 minutes to cool. Cover with plastic wrap and place in the fridge for at least 4 hours to set- should cool and very firm to touch. At this point it can be covered with plastic wrap and placed in the refrigerator for up to 3 days ahead to save time.
Preheat oven to 400 degrees.

Remove from refrigerator and cut into 12 equal pieces. If serving for a party or as an appetizer/first-course then cut each piece in half diagonally. Line the base of a large roasting pan with non-stick baking paper and arrange polenta pieces in a single layer with about 1/4 inch of space between. Drizzle over the oil and sprinkle with the extra parmesan cheese and fresh ground black pepper.
Bake in oven for 20 minutes or until the cheese turns a medium golden brown (roughly the color of the crust on a loaf of bread). Remove and let cool for 15-20 minutes. Top with Fennel Slaw (recipe in this book) and a drizzle of lemon scented olive oil (see note below). .

NOTE: SCENTED OLIVE OILS

I enjoy keeping scented olive oils on hand to use in cooking. You can scent olive oil with any essential oil. I particularly like using lemon. Add about 10 drops of lemon essential oil to about 4 ounces of high-quality extra virgin olive oil. Store in a bottle with a tight lid.

Orange Oil Poke

MARINATED TUNA

1 POUND AHI TUNA, LARGE DICED IN 1/4 TO 1/2 INCH CUBES
2 TABLESPOONS TOASTED SESAME OIL
3 DROPS ORANGE ESSENTIAL OIL
1 MEYER LEMON RIND, FINELY MINCED
1 TABLESPOON BLACK SESAME SEEDS
ONE PINCH TABASCO POWDER OR 1/4 TEASPOON TABASCO SAUCE

PONZU SAUCE

3 TEASPOONS FRESH OREGANO, MINCED
2 PINCHES BLACK LAVA SALT
1/4 CUP OLIVE OIL

1/2 CUP YUZU SAUCE
1 TEASPOON BLACK SESAME SEEDS
COMBINE ALL INGREDIENTS AND STIR WELL.

GARNISH

1 MEYER LEMON RIND, FINELY ZESTED
1 TABLESPOON MINT LEAVES, FINELY SLICED (CHIFFONADE)
COMBINE LEMON RIND AND MINT IN ICE WATER AND HOLD FOR GARNISH.

DIRECTIONS

Combine sesame oil, orange oil and tuna. Marinate for 30 minutes. Before serving, add lemon rind, tabasco, and sesame seeds and stir. Drizzle with ponzu sauce and garnish with lemon rind and mint leaves.

98

Zanzibar Rice Pilau

We travelled to Zanzibar Tanzania on safari one summer. While there I had the good fortune of taking a cooking class from a nice lady named Lutfia in her home. She taught me this traditional Swahili dish Rice Pilau. Zanzibar is known for growing spices so the dish she made was very fragrant with the fresh-grown spices she had available and local to Zanzibar. To recreate the dish in as aromatic and fragrant a form at home, I used essential oils to recreate the fresh spice aromas and flavors. You will love this!

– Chef John

INGREDIENTS

3 CUPS BASMATI RICE

6 CUPS WATER

2 OUNCES VEGETABLE OIL (PREFER COCONUT OIL)

1 MEDIUM RED ONION, SLICED

2 CLOVES GARLIC, MINCED AND CRUSHED TO A PUREE

2 OUNCES FRESH GINGER, MINCED AND CRUSHED TO A PUREE

3 TABLESPOONS SALT

1 WHOLE CINNAMON STICK

6 CARDAMOM PODS, CRUSHED

1 TABLESPOON BLACK PEPPERCORNS

1 TEASPOON FRESH GROUND CUMIN

2 TABLESPOONS BUTTER

2 DROPS CINNAMON BARK ESSENTIAL OIL

4 DROPS CARDAMOM ESSENTIAL OIL

2 DROPS BLACK PEPPER ESSENTIAL OIL

3 DROPS CUMIN ESSENTIAL OIL

DIRECTIONS

Preheat oven to 350 degrees F. Boil one cup of the water. Place whole cinnamon stick, cardamom pods, black peppercorns, and fresh ground cumin in a bowl. Pour boiling water over and let steep.

In heavy duty oven-proof 6-quart pot, heat oil and saute onions on medium high until light brown in color. Add ginger and garlic and saute for three more minutes. Add the entire contents of the bowl of spices, including liquid, heat and stir for about 2 minutes, until very fragrant.

Add rice and remaining water to the pot. Bring mix to a boil, then turn heat down to medium and cover. Simmer for 15 minutes, stirring every 2-3 minutes to make sure it doesn't stick. After 15 minutes, the rice should be thick but not soupy.

Place covered pot in the preheated oven for 15 more minutes. While baking, melt the butter and let cool slightly then add the oils to the butter. Refrigerate until ready to use. Remove rice from oven and add essential oil butter, stirring gently to incorporate. Taste and add salt to your taste preference.
Serves 5-6 generous portions.

NOTE ABOUT BASMATI RICE

Lutfia, a Zanzibar woman, taught me this recipe in her coooking school. I learned that Basmati rice is a staple of Zanzibar cuisine, grown locally on the island. Basmati is a long-grain rice with a delicate, light texture. Be careful not to overmix cooked Basmati or the finished product will resemble oatmeal with broken rice pieces. To purchase Basmati rice, look for "extra long grain" in cloth packaging. Also, Basmati rice is slightly brown in color, not white. The color results from the aging process that helps dry the rice to make it fluffier.

List of essential oils used in this book

BASIL ESSENTIAL OIL

BAY LAUREL ESSENTIAL OIL

BLACK PEPPER ESSENTIAL OIL

CARDAMOM ESSENTIAL OIL

CILANTRO ESSENTIAL OIL

CINNAMON BARK ESSENTIAL OIL

CLOVE ESSENTIAL OIL

CORIANDER ESSENTIAL OIL

CUMIN ESSENTIAL OIL

DILL ESSENTIAL OIL

FENNEL ESSENTIAL OIL

GINGER ESSENTIAL OIL

LAVENDER ESSENTIAL OIL

LEMON ESSENTIAL OIL

LEMONGRASS ESSENTIAL OIL

LIME ESSENTIAL OIL

NUTMEG ESSENTIAL OIL

ORANGE ESSENTIAL OIL

OREGANO ESSENTIAL OIL

PARSLEY ESSENTIAL OIL

PEPPERMINT ESSENTIAL OIL

ROSEMARY ESSENTIAL OIL

SAGE ESSENTIAL OIL

THYME ESSENTIAL OIL

Notes

Notes

Notes

Made in the USA
Las Vegas, NV
04 December 2020

12045538R00069